Ali Albashir M. Alhaj

Syntax

An Introduction: A Textbook for University students of Linguistics & Translation

Anchor Academic
Publishing

Alhaj, Ali Albashir M.: Syntax: An Introduction: A Textbook for University students of Linguistics & Translation, Hamburg, Anchor Academic Publishing 2015

Buch-ISBN: 978-3-95489-889-3
PDF-eBook-ISBN: 978-3-95489-381-2
Druck/Herstellung: Anchor Academic Publishing, Hamburg, 2015

Bibliografische Information der Deutschen Nationalbibliothek:
Die Deutsche Nationalbibliothek verzeichnet diese Publikation in der Deutschen Nationalbibliografie; detaillierte bibliografische Daten sind im Internet über http://dnb.d-nb.de abrufbar.

Bibliographical Information of the German National Library:
The German National Library lists this publication in the German National Bibliography. Detailed bibliographic data can be found at: http://dnb.d-nb.de

© Anchor Academic Publishing, Imprint der Diplomica Verlag GmbH
Hermannstal 119k, 22119 Hamburg
http://www.diplomica-verlag.de, Hamburg 2015
Printed in Germany

CHAPTER ONE

BASIC IDEAS IN SYNTAX

"…Syntax begins when morphology ends…"

Huddleston(1986: 90)

1.1 Defining Syntax:

Syntax can be defined as:

1. the study of how words combine to form sentences and the rules which govern the formation of sentences.
2. the second part of grammar, that teaches the construction of words.(Hertord el al 1970:528).
3. the internal structure of a unit of grammatical analysis.
4. the analysis of the structure of phrases and sentences.
5. the study of sentence structure.
6. the study of the rules governing the ways words are combined.

1.2 Is Syntax Opposed to Morphology?

Syntax deals with units of a much higher rank than those which are studied in morphology. In this use, syntax is opposed to morphology, the study of word structure. In that sense, Chomsky (1971) at al claims that the principles that regulate the internal structure of words are quite different from those that govern sentence structure, the domain of syntax. Some of the major differences are summarized by katamba (1992: 217):-

Morphology	Syntax
(1).Lexical rules may relate items from different word-classes (e.g., derive adverbs from adjectives.	(1).Syntactic rules do not change
(2)Lexical rules apply to the output of other lexical	Word-classes.

Morphology	Syntax
rules but not to the output of syntactic rules (e.g., develop{v},→ develop{v}+ment{n}→development{n}+al){adj}→ developmental){adj}. (3) Lexical rules may have arbitrary lexical exceptions (e.g., normally an agentive noun can be derived from a verb by suffixing {-er}.However, this is not allowed if the verb is(spy) (*spier) (4)Lexical rules use recursion only to a limited extent .(words like great-great –great- great-great - great-great –aunt) , while not rule out, are decidedly odd. (5) Morphology has paradigms.	(2).Syntactic rules have access to the output of both lexical and syntactic. (3) Syntactic rules do not have arbitrary lexical expressions(such as the passivisation of a sentence being blocked if the subject NP contains the noun *safari*, because that word is borrowed from Swahili). (4) Recursion is extensively used in syntax. (5) Syntax has no paradigms.

1.3 What are the Two Kinds of Rules in Modern Syntax.?

There are two kinds of rules in modern Syntax.

A) Phrase Structure Rules:

Phrase Structure(PS) rules have two main functions in Syntax

(i) to describe the internal composition of larger syntactic units or categories.

(ii) the ordering **between** smaller units that make up phrases .

B) Transformational Rules:

Transformational rules serve to map the deep structure on the surface Structure. They serve account for surface differences between meaning-related sentences, such as passive-active sentence .

E.g.,

- Ali broke the door.
- The door was broken by Ali.(Linguistic File.p,.24).

1.4 What is the Difference between Surface Structure and Deep Structure?

According to Richard (2001:99): in earlier models of transformational grammar, each sentence was considered to have two levels of structure: the deep structure and the surface structure.

- In traditional grammar, a sentence like (**Ali broke the door**) is called an active sentence, focusing on what Ali did, however, a sentence like(**The door was broken by Ali**.) is a passive sentence, focusing on (**the door**)and what happened to it

- To capture the facts just examined in sentence like the above-mentioned examples, we postulate two levels of sentence structure. One level is represented by the linear string of words as uttered or written. It is called **the surface structure**.(**S. structure**.) Surface structure encompasses both the linear order of the constituents and their hierarchical order.

- The deep structure (**D. structure**) is much more abstract and is considered to be in the speaker's, writer's, hearer's or reader's mind. The deep structure for the above sentence would be something like:
  - It was Ali who broke the door.
  - Was the door broken by Ali?

Yule(2004:88) has pointed out that"' the deep structure is an abstract level of structural organization in which all the elements determining structural interpretations are represented .

1.5 What Is a Sentence?

A sentence can be defined as:-

(1) a group of words expressing a complete thought.

(2) an utterance which makes just as long a communication as the speaker has intended to make before giving himself.

(3) a grammatically constructed smallest unit of speech which express its content with respect to this content's relation to reality.

(4) a portion of speech that is putting forward to the listener a state of things (a thing meant) as having validity ,i.e., as being true.

(5) a (relatively)complete and independent human utterance – the completeness and independence being shown by its standing alone or its capability of standing alone, i.e., of being uttered by itself.

(6) a group of words joined together by grammatical agreements { relating devices} and which, not grammatically dependent upon any other group, are complete in themselves .

(7) a construction (or from0 which in the given utterance , is not part of any larger construction.

(8) a group of words, phrases or clauses that can occur in isolation. (as quoted in Fries 1980:20).

(9) A group of words with two main parts: a complete subject and a complete predicate. Together these parts express a complete thought.

1.6 The Four Structures of Sentence.

The four basic sentence structures are:

(i) **Simple Sentence** :-

A sentence which contains only one predicate or a single independent clause

E.g., **a**. I <u>like milk.</u>

B. The <u>Winter arrived</u> early.

C. Struck by novelty of the idea, Dr.<u>Ali grinned</u> with pleasure.

(ii) **Compound Sentence** :-

A sentence which contains two or more independent clauses which are joined by –co-ordination.

E.g., **a**. Dr. <u>Ali</u> <u>went</u> to a moll this morning, but <u>he</u> <u>did</u> not <u>buy</u> anything.

b. <u>Ahmed is a young boy</u>, but <u>he is very clever</u>.

   (ind. Clause)   (ind. Clause)

A. <u>Khalid</u> <u>is</u> a night owl; therefore. <u>He</u> <u>sleeps</u> late in the morning.

(iii) Complex Sentence :-

A sentence which contains one or more dependent or subordinate clauses, in addition to its independent , or main,

E.g., **a**. <u>Whoever</u> <u>wants</u> this job <u>can have</u>.

       (Main Clause Subordinate Clause)

   b. <u>When it rained,</u> <u>we went inside</u> .

    (Dep. Clause)   (ind. Clause)

   c.   <u>Ali said</u>, the <u>car broke</u>.

(iv) Compound Complex Sentence:-

A sentence which consists of two or more independent clauses and one or more subordinate clauses.

E.g., **a**. The <u>truck dropped</u> its load of gravel onto the
          Driveway (ind. Clause)

    Where the <u>car was parked</u>, and then the <u>truck drove</u> off.

    (subordinate clause)   (independent clause)

   b. When the <u>lights went</u> out, <u>we felt</u> extremely uneasy, (subordinate clause)   (independent clause)

But we always <u>knew</u> that <u>morning would</u> eventually <u>come</u>.

(independent clause)   (subordinate clause)

1.7   The Four Functions of Sentences

Sentences may also be classified by function. According to Aiken(19981:15)"
according to their idea or content English sentences are classified as declarative,
interrogative, imperative, or exclamatory. The first makes a statement, the second
asks a question, the third makes a request , and the fourth expresses strong
emotion."

(i)   <u>Declarative Sentence</u> :

A declarative sentence states an idea and ends with a period or full stop.

E.g.,

    a. All of tries are new.

    b. Dr. Ali is an expert in translation.

    C. Ahmed doesn't like sweet things.

(ii)   <u>Interrogative Sentence:</u>

An interrogative sentence asks a question and ends with a question
mark.

E.g.,

a. Did you renew your newspaper subscription?(Yes/no questions)

b. You renew your newspaper subscription?(Intonation).

c.   When did you renew your newspaper subscription

(iii)   Imperative Sentence:

An imperative sentence gives an order or a direction and ends with a period or an exclamation mark.

E.g.,

a. Come here.

b. Run!

c. will someone please take these packages into the
house before drop them!

(iv)   Exclamatory Sentence:

An exclamatory sentence conveys emotion and ends with an exclamation mark.

E.g.,

a. Would you look at that!

b. What a terrible noise!

c. How wonderful!

1.8   The Three Basic Properties of Sentence Structures.

Jacobs (2001:35) listed the following three majors properties of sentence structure

1. **Linearity**: Sentences are produced and received in a linear sequence.

2. Hierarchy: Sentences are hierarchically structured, that is, they are not simply sequences of individual words but are made up of word groupings, which themselves may consist of lesser groups.

3.   **Categorically**: Sentences are made up of parts which belong to a set of distinct categories, each with its special characteristics.   (Jacobs.pp.35-40 for further reading and more details) .

1.9   Basic Sentence Patterns

There are five basic pattern for sentence with complement

No	Patterns	Examples
1	S-AV-DO	Dr. Ali delivered a fascinating Lecture.
2	S-AV-IO-DO	Her father wrote her a letter.
3	S-AV-DO- OC	My daughter success made me happy.
4	S-LV-PN	Cobra is a poisonous snake.
5	S-LV-PA	Ahmed is ill today.

1.10   Negative Sentences Correctly

Negative sentences are formed correctly in one f the three ways:-

(1)Using One Negative Word :-

The most common way to take a statement negative is with a single negative word, such is(**no, not, none, nothing, never, nobody, or nowhere**, or with the contraction- **n't**)added to a helping verb.

Note: DO NOT USE TWO NEHATIVE WORDS IN THE SAME CLAUSE.

Using two of these negative words in the same clause will create a double negative. Jacobs (ibid.272).

E.g.,

- **Double Negative:-** He hasn't never told us the truth.
- **Correct:-** He has never told us the truth.

(2)Using (But) in a Negative Sense:-

When (but) means "**only**", it usually acts as a negative.

Note: DO NOT USE BUT IN ITS NEGATIVE SENSE WITH AN OTHER NEGATIVE.

E.g.,

- **Double Negative:-** She didn't offer *but* one reasonable excuse.
- **Correct:-** She offered *but* one reasonable excuse.
- **Correct:** She offered **only** one reasonable excuse. Jacobs (ibid.p,272) .

(3) Using (*Barley, Hardly, and Scarcely*):-

These words have a negative sense and should not be used with other negative words.

Note: DO NOT USE BARLEY, SCARCELY HARDLY, WITH AN OTHER NEGATIVE.

- **Double Negative:-** He wasn't *barley* able to recognize her.
- **Correct:-** He was *barely* able to recognize her.
- **Double Negative:-** The motorist couldn't *hardly* see the traffic light.
- **Correct:-** The motorist could *hardly* see the traffic light.
- **Double Negative:-** The lecture hadn't *scarcely* begun.
- **Correct** The lecture had *scarcely* begun.

Practice Exercise (1)

PART ONE

i. **Define the following terms?**

    a. Syntax...

    ....

    b. Surfacestructure...

    ....

    c. InterrogativeSentence...

    ....

    d. Exclamatory Sentence..

    e. Imperative Sentence...

    f. Declarative Sentence...

    g. Linearity:...

    h. Categorically...

ii. **Use the following instructions to write ten sentences of your own.**

    a. Write a simple declarative sentence.

    ....

    b. Write a compound declarative sentence.

    ....

    ....

    c. Write a simple interrogative sentence.

    ....

    ....

    d. Write a compound interrogative sentence.

    ....

    ....

e. Write a simple exclamatory sentence.

…………………………………………………………………………………………

…………………………………………………………………………..

f. Write a complex declarative sentence.

…………………………………………………………………………………………

…………………………………………………………………………………..

g. Write a complex interrogative sentence.

…………………………………………………………………………………………

…………………………………………………………………………..

h. Write a compound- complex declarative sentence.

…………………………………………………………………………………………

…………………………………………..

i. Write a compound- complex interrogative sentence.

…………………………………………………………………………………………

…………………………………………………………………………….

PART TWO

i.   What are the two kinds of rules in modern Syntax?

…………………………………………………………………………………………

…………………………………………………..

ii.   What are the three basic properties of sentence structures?

…………………………………………………………………………………………

………………………………………………………………………………………

iii.   What are the four functions of sentence?

…………………………………………………………………………………………

……………………………………………………..

iv.   What are the four structures of sentence?

…………………………………………………………………………………………

………………………………………………………………………………………

v. What is the difference between surface structure and deep structure?

....

....

PART THREE

Find the subordinate clauses in these sentences:

i. A bee performs a special dance, when it has found, to inform the others.

....

....

ii. Most employees will be happy if the regulation to reduce work hours is passed

....

....

iii. The book fair which was opened yesterday visited by many students.

....

....

iv. Many people came to California in the 1860s believing that they would find gold

....

....

v. Although we call them shooting stars, meteorites are bit of matter from other planets entering the earth's atmosphere

....

....

PART FOUR

State whether each of the following sentences is declarative, imperative, interrogative or exclamatory.

i. What a fool

....

ii. What is he doing?

……………………...

iii. Aren't you coming with us?

………………………………....................................

iv. Water boils at 100 degree centigrade

……………………………………………………………

v. Who on earth painted that

vi. E. Hemingway, a novelist and short- story writer, developed a prose style…………………………………

vii. I don't know why he said that………..………………

CHAPTER TWO

NOUNS & PRONOUNS IN ENGLISH

The investigation of words is the beginning of Education

A.S. Conran.

2.1 Defining Nouns

Nouns can be defined as :-

i.   the name of a person, animal, place, concept or thing.

ii. naming things that can be seen and touched as well as those that cannot be seen and touched.

According to Jarvie(1990:9) traditionally, nouns are defined as " naming words', or the names of persons, animals, places or things/. This is still a useful definition, as far as it goes. But modern grammarians are interested in describing the function of a word, as well as defining its meaning. They like to clarify what a word does in a sentence before assigning a part of speech to it. For example, look at the nouns in these

a. Stop the watch!

b. They threw out the rubbish.

c. Watch the stop!

d. They rubbished his throw.

2.2 Defining Pronouns

Pronoun can be defined as:-

i.   set of items which can be used to substitute for a single noun or noun phrase.

ii. a word that stands for a nouns ,or a noun phrase ,or something relating to it.

iii. Words that stand for nouns or for words those take the place of nouns.

2.3   Differences between Nouns and Pronouns.

Thakur(ibid.p.,3) listed the following differences between nouns and pronouns:-

i.   Nouns do not have contrasting case forms as some pronouns have. The noun _student_, for example, can be used as a subject, as an object or as a completive to a preposition without any morphological change. This is not true about the central members of the pronominal class. Nominative forms like _he_, _she_, and _we_, for example, cannot occur in the position of an object or in the position of a completive to a preposition without any morphological change.   Similarly, the accusative forms like _him_, _her_, _me_ and _us_ cannot occur in the position of the subject of a sentence.

ii.   The majority of nouns can be changed into their plural forms by the addition of the inflectional suffix {-s} or {-es}.Pronouns are not amendable to such morphological changes indicating plurality. It is true that many pronouns have their singular as well as plural forms but in most cases (as in _I/ we, he/ they, she/they, it/they, me/us and my/our)_ their plural forms cannot be predicted in terms of a morphological rule.

iii.   Pronouns cannot take all the premodifiers   that nouns can. They cannot, for example, co-occur with the indefinite articles _a_ or _an_. The indefinite pronouns _one_ can be preceded by _the_, but the central members of this class cannot be   preceded by the definite article. Except in phrases like " _poor old you"_ pronouns cannot be preceded by adjectives either.

2.4   Count nouns and Non-count nNouns

a. Count nouns refer to entities viewed in English as individual units. They are sometimes described as having the feature (+count). The entities they refer to can be abstract (an idea, suggestions, belief, prejudice) as well as concrete (a house, child, potatoes, finger).Jacobs, ibid.106).

b. Noncount nouns typically refer to entities that are viewed not as individual units but as something having no specific shape or boundary . They are described as having the negative value for count feature {- count.} Jacobs, ibid.106).

c. Quirk(ibid,p.,60) listed the following some examples which are non-count in English but count nouns in some other languages:

Anger, applause, behavior, chaos, homework, poetry, parking, safety, moonlight, research, chess, leisure, smoking, progress, harm, education, photography, weather, sunshine, conduct, etc...

d. Nouns are countable if:

- o they can be preceded by a: a bus.
- o They can be both singular and plural: a cat, cats.
- o They can be counted: one taxi, two taxis, twenty taxis.

e. Nouns are uncountable if:

- o They are preceded by some rather than a: some salt, some marmalade.
- o They are not normally counted or pluralized: two butters, eleven flours.
- o Most uncountable nouns denote commodities or notions that tend not to be counted out as individual objects. We say *two organs* or *six apples*(countable), but we don't normally say *two butters* or *six breads* (uncountable.) For uncountable commodities we have to bring in other forms of measurements, such as:
  - A bag/spoonful/ton of flour.
  - One/two /three grains of sand.
  - A piece of information/music.
  - A slice of bread/cake/cake/beef.
  - A ton of rice/cement/rubbish.
  - An ounce of curry power.

f. Occasionally, nouns may be either countable or uncountable, depending on the context, such as:

  - I need a pound of sugar.(uncountable).
  - One sager or two.(countable).

- I never eat cake.(uncountable).

2.5   Collective Nouns or Mass Nouns

Collective can be defined as:-

- A noun which refers to a collection of people, animals, or things, as a group. For example, school, family, government.
- Collective nouns refer to groups of animate beings, such as class, committee, council, government or herd.
- Collective nouns are singular nouns, but they carry a plural connotation. They are used when the whole group or gathering is being considered (rather than individual members of the group).
- Being singular, collective nouns usually take singular verbs or pronouns. E.g.

The committee {has/ have met and{it has/they have) rejected the proposal .

N.B:- the use of the plural verb suggests that the noun refers to something which is seen as a group of individuals, whereas the use of the singular verb suggests something seen as a single whole.

According to Jacobs (ibid,p.,114):-

… One last significant problem for classification concerns collective nouns, which refer to groups of individuals. In American and Canadian English, when singular nouns like administrative, government, public, crowd, committee, audience, are used as subjects, present tense verbs are almost inevitably in their singular form, while in British plural forms also occur frequently, especially when the members of the group are being viewed as individuals rather than as an undifferentiated grouping:-

a. The government has announced a new initiative (American)
b. The government has/has announced a new initiative. (British).

We may distinguish three subclasses of collective nouns:-

a. **Specific**: army, clan, class, club, committee, crew, crowd, family, flock. gang, government, group, herd, jury, majority, minority .

b. **Generic:** the elite, the gentry, the laity, the public.

c. **Unique:** The Arab league, (the) Congress, Parliament, the United Nation, the United Nation.

2.6 A Stock Collective Nouns Specific to Certain Animals & Groups.

There is a large stock collective nouns specific to certain animals and groups .Some of the best known include:

1. A fleet of ships.
2. A herd of cattle.
3. A flock of birds.
4. A crowd of people.
5. A pack of wolves.
6. A bunch of keys.
7. A flight of stairs.
8. School/shoal offish.
9. A bunch of grapes.
10. A gang of thieves.
11. A pack of cards.
12. Crew /airmen of sailors.

2.7 Compound Nouns

Compound noun is a noun that is made of more than one word.

There are three types of compound nouns:-

i.   **Separated:-**

E.g. Fire, soap.

ii.   **Hyphenated:**

E.g., commander-in-chief.

Jack-of-all-trades.

iii. Combined :

E.g., toothbrush. Dishwasher.

Compounds form the plural different ways, but(c) below is the most usual:-

a. **Plural in first element:-**

E.g.,
- Passer-by= passers -by.
- Mother-in-law= mothers-in-law.

b. **Plural in both first and last element** :-

E.g.,
- Woman doctor=woman doctors.
- Gentleman farmer= gentlemen farmer.

c. **Plural in last element:-**

E.g.,
- Assistant professors.
- Assistant directors.

2.8 Types of Pronouns .

There six forms of pronouns in English: Personal Pronouns, Reflexive Pronouns, Distributive Pronouns, Possessive Pronouns, Object Pronouns, Relative Pronouns.

a. Personal Pronouns:-

- Personal pronouns function as replacement for co-referential noun phases in neighboring (usually preceding) clauses.
- Personal pronouns refer to **(1)** the person speaking**, (2)** the person spoken to, or**(3)** the person**,** place, or thing spoken about**.**

Type of person	Singular	Plural
First person	I, me, my, mine.	We, us, our, ours.
Second person	You, your, yours.	You, yours, your.
Third person	He, him, his, she, her, hers, it, its.	They, them, their, theirs

b. Reflexive_and intensive Pronouns

- Reflexive pronouns replace a co-referential noun phrase, normally within the same finite verb clause.
- A reflexive pronoun ends in –self or-self and adds information to a sentence by pointing back to a noun or pronoun earlier in the sentence.
- An intensive pronoun ends in-self or-selves and simply adds emphasis to a noun or pronoun in the same sentence.
- The reflexive pronoun is used:
  a. As the object of a verb when the subject and the object are the same person.
     o He serves *himself* at the café.
     o She cut *herself* while cooking.
  b. For emphasis. It follows the subject verb before a preposition and means the subject did the action alone.
     o I looked *myself* for the missing keys.

     Otherwise it goes at the end of the sentence.

     o I made this shirt *myself*.
     o You told me *yourself*.
  c. After the preposition " by" .It means that the subject did the action alone.
     o He like to shop *himself*.

o My little daughter has learnt to use computer *by herself.*

Type of person	Singular	Plural
First person	Myself	Ourselves
Second person	Yourself	Yourselves
Third person	Himself, herself, itself	Themselves

c. **Distributive Pronouns.**

- They refer to members of a group or class.
- There are six of these in English, namely 'all', 'both', 'each',' either,' neither', 'and 'some'.
- Often, these pronouns are followed by phrases, such as ' of you' or' of them'.
  - All (of you) will go.
  - Both (of you) should come.
  - Each (of them) will receive $100.
  - Either (of you) will do.
  - Either (of them) can read or write properly.
  - Some (of you) will have to go.

d. **Possessive Pronouns**

The possessive pronouns belong to two series:

- The attributives (my, your, etc..). which are systemically determiners
- Nominals (mine, yours, etc,,) which are used like the genitive with ellipsis. Compare:
  - Mary's book. → – the book is Mary's.
  - Her book → - the book is hers.
- The possessive pronoun is used :-

A) to replace a possessive adjective + a noun. Instead of saying" This book in <u>my book</u>". we say ," This book is <u>mine.</u>"

E.g.,

- Our van is big, and *theirs*(their van) is small.
- His score was good but *her*(her score*)* was better.

B) after the preposition "of ", when it indicates " one of several".

- Dr. Ali is a colleague of *mine* (one of several colleagues).
- I met a teacher of *yours* yesterday.(one of several teachers).

C) after the verb " to be":

- That car is *mine*.
- Is this notebook is *yours*?

D) to replace the second adjective +noun when comparing two objects:

- His grades are better than *theirs.*(their grades).
- His farm is bigger than *yours*(your farm).

E.) **Object Pronouns**

The object pronoun is used:

i. **when it is the direct object of a verb:**

- He gave *her* his new book.
- They saw *him* in class.

ii. **when the objects of two clauses are compared:-**

- They worry about *you* more than *him*.
- The office staff helped *you* more than(they helped) *me*.

iii. **After prepositions :**

- Ali studies English with *us.*
- It did not sound like a good ideas to *me*.

N.B. if the preposition introduces a new clause, the subject pronoun must be used because it is the subject of the new clause.

- They left after *he* called.

f. Relative Pronouns

The relative pronouns are structure words which convert sentence patterns into adjective clauses. A relative pronoun does several jobs:

1. It converts the sentence pattern it introduces into a clause within another sentence.
2. Within its clause, it performs the function (subject, object, or modifier) of the word or words it is replacing.
3. Most important, it ties the whole structure, the clause, to the preceding noun.

Al- Hamash(1978:190) introduces each one of these relative pronouns, and states that adjective clause may be introduced by a relative pronoun, a relative conjunction, or a relative determiner, which as a whole a whole can be called " relatives", with its reference.

Pronoun	Use
Who	People+ household animals
Whom	People+ household animals
Which	Things
That	All nouns
Whose	All nouns

- **Who**: is used in subject positions and it refers to animate nouns.

  E.g. The boy who won the contest is my student.
- **Whom :** is used in object position and refers to people.

  E.g. I met my friend whom I like.

- **Which:** refers to things, collective nouns. And animals.

  E.g., It was a fascinating lecture, *which* I never forget.

- **That :** refers to people, things, and animals.

  E.g. The police arrested the burglar *that* we were afraid of.

- **Whose:** refers to animals, people, and things and indicates possession.

  E.g. Here's the boy *whose* car was stolen

Practice Exercise (2)

PART ONE

A. Fill each blank with the correct collective noun from the following box :

Carillon	Gang	Company	Horde	Crowd
Drove	Audience	Congregation	Litter	Brood
School	Shoal	Team	Pack	Troop
Nest	Skein	Gaggle	Herd	Flock

1. A……….of ponies.

2. A.......... of sheep.

3. A……….of cattle.

4. A……….of geese.(on the ground)

5. A……….of geese(when flying).

6. A………. of rabbits/ants/vipers.

7. A……….of lions/monkeys/cavalry/fairies.

8. A………of wolves/hounds/submarines.

9. A……….of oxen/mules/horses.

10.A………..of herring/mackerel.

11.A………. of whales/ porpoises.

12.A……….of chickens.

13.A……….of puppies/kittens/piglets.

14.A………. of moll-people.

15.A……… of concert -goers.

16. A……….of spectators.

17.A……….of savages.

18.A…………of actors/artists.

19.A………..of workmen/prisoners.

20.A……….of bell.

B. Identifying Personal, Reflexive, and Intensive Pronouns. Write the pronoun in each sentence. Then label each as personal, reflexive/or intensive.

1) Father wrote you an intriguing letter last month.

   ………………………………………………………………….

2) They served themselves in the cafeteria.

   ………………………………………………………………….

3) I can't study while the radio is playing.

   …………………………………………………………………

4) The captain himself is coming to launch the ship.

   ……………………………………………………………………

5) The sun itself provides energy, light, and warmth.

   …………………………………………………………………..

PART TWO

A. Correct the pronouns in these sentences where necessary.

1. Could you explain this matter to me?

   ……………………………………………………………….

2. Ali sat between Ahmed and I.

   ……………………………………………………………….

3. I go with they to the cafeteria.

   …………………………………………………………………

4. Between you and I, I didn't like the food.

   …………………………………………………………………

5. What is the matter with he?

   …………………………………………………………………....

B. Fill in the blanks with a possessive pronoun:

1. I've mislaid my pencil. May I borrow……..?

2. Dr. Ishaq wants you to return that book of…….which you borrowed last month.

3. We had a test too, but yours was harder than……

4. Is this your car? Yes, it's………

5. I was on time for my class but Ali was late for……

PART THREE

1. Two pronouns/adjectives are underlined in each sentence. Indicate which of them is not correct. A or B.

a) The team has finished its season with another victory for their supporters...............................

b) Neither Ali nor his friends received his test scores.............

c) Every discount store advertises that their products are cheaper than its competitors ....

d) His parents told them to put his coat on...............

e) Someone has forgotten to put their name on his term paper..........

2. Fill each blanks with the correct word from the box below

Grain	Chip	Drop
Pinch	Blade	Flash
Scrap	Speck	Lock
Breath	Dash	Fragment

a) A............. of salt.

b) A..............of rain.

c) A..............of hair.

d) A..............of paper.

e) A...............of air.

f) A............of lighting.

g) A.............of grass.

h) A.............of pepper.

i) A.............of sand.

j) A.............of dirt.

k) A............of wood.

l) A...........of glass.

PART FOUR

1. **Which of these nouns are typically used as count nouns and which as non count nouns:**

   a. Money……………………………………………………..

   b. Sugar……………………………………………………..

   c. Envy……………………………………………………….

   d. Culture…………………………………………………….

   e. Turf………………………………………………………..

   f. Water………………………………………………………

   g. Pens…………………………………………………………

   h. Books………………………………………………………

   i. Victory……………………………………………………

   j. Recession …………………………………………………

2. Give the plural of these nouns:

   a. Sand………………………………………………………...

   b. Postage……………………………………………………..

   c. Progress……………………………………………………

   d. Evidence……………………………..…………………….

   e. Age…………………………………………………………

   f. Soap………………………………….……………………

   g. Tea…………………………………………………………

CHAPTER THREE

VERB &VERB PHRASES IN ENGLISH

A word is dead, when it is said, some said. I say it just. Begins to live. That day.

Emily Dickinson

3.1   Defining Verb.

A verb can be defined as:

i.   A word that expresses time while showing an action, a condition or the fact that something.

ii.   A word which,(**i**) occurs as part of the predicate of a sentence(**ii**) carries markers of grammatical categories such as tense, aspect, person, number and mood, and(**iii**) refers to an action or state.

E.g.

- She opened the window.
- Children like chocolate.

3.2   The two main kinds of Verb.

a) Action verbs:

- an action verb is a verb that tells what action someone or something is performing.

E.g.,

- Dr. Ali thought deeply about the issue.
- Ahmed painted the tool shed.

- An action verb is transitive if it directs action toward someone or something named in the same sentence.

- An action verb is intransitive if it does not direct action toward someone or something named in the same sentence.

E.g.,
- Columbus discovered America (transitive verb.
- Dr. Sameeh waited for the bus(intransitive)

b) Linking verbs (copula).

1. A linking verb is a verb that connects a word at or near the beginning of a sentence with a word at or near the end.   To quote Quirk(ibid.,p.,353): there is intensive complementation of the verb when a subject complement is present . The verb in such a sentence is a 'copula' or' linking verb' the most common copula is{be}.

E.g.,

- There <u>are</u> several mistakes in his essays.
- The weather <u>is</u> horrible.
- At sunset the sky <u>was</u> cloudy.

The most common liking verbs are listed below:-

Appear	Feel	Look
Remain	Seem	Smell
Sound	Taste	Become
Get	Go	Grow
Turn	Make	Stay

3. The chief patterns of linking verbs are:-
   a. Subject +linking verb+ Adjective (phrase).

   E.g., The headmaster <u>is</u> busy.
   b. Subject +linking verb+ noun phrase.

E.g., basketball <u>is</u> my favorite sport.

  c. Subject +linking verb+ adverbial.

    E.g., This place <u>is</u> where my friend's father died .

  d. Subject+ verb+ to be +complement.

    E.g., Dr. Ali <u>seems to be</u> an excellent freelance translator.

  e. Subject+ verb+ like+ noun phrase.

    E.g., The object <u>looked like</u> a flying saucer.

  f. Subject+ verb+ as if +clause.

    E.g., the milk <u>tastes as</u> if it has been boiled.

3.3 Active and Passive.

  1) Voice can be defined

- the form of a verb that shows whether the subject is performing the action.
- The ways in which a language expresses the relationship between a verb and the noun phrase which are associated with it. Two sentences can differ in voice and yet have the same basic meaning. However, there may be a change in emphasis and one type of sentence may be more appropriate.

  E.g.,

    ○ The cat chased the mouse. {active}

    ○ The mouse was chased (by the cat) {Passive}.

  2) Active voice can be defined as:

- A verb is active if its subject performs the action.

  E.g., The wind damaged the fence.

  E.g., The fence was damaged by the wind.

3) The passive voice is used to emphasize the receiver of an action rather than the performer of an action.

E.g.,

Peter Newmark was awarded the Prize by the British Association of Applied Linguistics in 1988.

4) The passive voice is used to point the receiver of an action whenever the performer is not important or not easily identified.

E.g.,

The nuclear material was removed to a safe location.

3.4 Main Forms of the Passive Verb Phrase.

o A passive verb is made from a form of (be) plus the past participle of a transitive.

Active	Passive
• The researcher <u>surfs</u> the Net • The researcher <u>is surfing</u> the Net • The researcher <u>has surfed</u> the Net.	• The Net is surfed by the researcher. • The Net is being surfed by the researcher. • The Net has been surfed by the researcher.
• The researcher <u>surfed</u> the Net. • The researcher was <u>surfing</u> the Net. • The researcher <u>had surfed</u> the Net. • The researcher <u>will surf</u> the Net. • The researcher <u>is going to surf</u> the Net.	• The Net was surfed by the researcher. • The Net was being surfed by the researcher. • The Net had been surfed by the researcher.

Active	Passive
	• The Net will be surfed by the researcher. • The Net is going to be surfed by the researcher.

3.5 Differences between Active& Passive Voice.

Jacobs(ibid. p.,160) listed the following three major differences between the active:

1. The verb in the active voice clause is its ordinary past tense form (surfed), whereas in the passive voice clause the verb unit is a sequence of a form of the copular verb be plus the past participle (surfed).

2. A verb is active if its subject performs the action.

3. A verb is passive if its action is perfumed upon the subject.

3.6 Subject and Verb agreement.

Subject –verb agreement presents difficulty to most learners of English since some subjects take a singular verb, some may take either a singular or plural verb, and some take a plural verb.

1. **Subject which take a singular verb(plural-looking Nouns):-**

   - Some common words ending in-s take a singular verb.
   - Nouns that are plural in form but singular in meaning agree with singular verbs.

Ethics	News	Semitics	Semantics
Physics	Measles	Mathematics	Series
Politics	Acoustics	Statistics	Semiotics
Mumps	Economics	Spaghetti	Esthetics
Acoustics	Alms	Aeronautics	Linguistics
Analytics	Athletics	Bellows	Civics
Comics	Dynamics	Ethics	Hydraulics
Hydromechanics	Magnetic	Metaphysics	Molasses
Mumps	Optics	Phonetics	Phonics
Pneumatics	Poetics	Rickets	Tactics

E.g.,

1. No news is a good news .
2. Semantics is a fascinating and intriguing subject.

2. **Subject which take a plural verb:**

- A compound subject joined by (and) is generally plural and must have a plural verb**.**

E.g.,

- Vegetables <u>and</u> fruit <u>are </u>good for you.
- Both my sister <u>and</u> my brother <u>are</u> here.

- The word "several", "both", "many" and "few" always take a plural verb:

E.g.,

- <u>Many</u> <u>are </u>volunteering to help.
- A few have failed the test.

3. Amounts and measurements:

A noun expressing an amount or measurement is usually singular and requires a singular verb.

E.g.,

- <u>Half</u> of the chickens <u>were sold.</u>
- <u>Three quarters</u> of the bushel of fruit was wasted.
- <u>Four feet was</u> the height of the chain link fence.

4. Subjects which may take either a singular verb or a plural verb.

- Some nouns take a singular verb when the phrase " pair of" or "word of" is included, but take a plural verb when these words are not included:

-

Pants	Shorts	Glasses
Thanks	Trousers	Jeans
Pliers	Means	

E.g.,

- These glasses <u>are</u> now.
- This pair of glasses <u>is</u> new.
- Many thanks were given.
- A word of thanks was given.

- Collective nouns take a singular verb when the group it names acts as a single unit.
- A collective noun takes a plural verb when the group it names act as individuals with different points of view.
- The following are some collective nouns:

Audience	Class	Couple	Crowd
Family	Faculty	Group	Orchestra
Team	Majority	Choir	Gang

E.g.,

- Our team <u>is</u> winning.(the team as a group).

  (singular)
- The team <u>are</u> going back to their homes.(meaning individual members). (plural)
- The jury <u>have</u> been unable to agree on a verdict. (plural)
- The faculty <u>have</u> been discussing the new policy. (plural)
- The orchestra <u>is</u> playing the national symphony. (singular)

5. Nouns for nationality ending in (-ese,-ch,-sh).

Nouns for nationality ending in(-ese,-ch,-sh) { for example, Japanese, Chinese, Vietnamese, French, English) take a singular verb when referring to a language , but a plural verb+ the when referring to the people:

E.g.,

- Japanese <u>is</u> a difficult language to write.
- The Japanese <u>are </u>famous for their beautiful gardens.
- French <u>is</u> spoken in parts of Canada.
- The French are known for their gastronomy.

Practical Exercise (3)

PART ONE

1) **Change these sentences from active into passive:**

   a. The students will receive the timetables next day.

   ………………………………………………….,……

   b. The academic advisor has seen the students..

   ………………………………………………….………

   c. Lighting hits many tall building.

   …………………………………………………….

   d. Dr. Ali is writing a book syntax& Morphology.

   …………………………………………………….

   e. The police caught the thief.

   …………………………………………………..

2) **Choose the correct form of the verb from the   parentheses:**

   a. All of money (was/were) found …………………….………

   b. My new pair of pants (is/are) at the cleaners…………….

   c. Both corn and wheat (is/are) grown in Sudan……….…....

   d. The Chinese (is/are) difficult language to study. ………

   e. number of graduates(have/has) receive scholarship from Jazan University.

PART TWO

1. Choose the correct form from the parentheses:

a. Every participant (has/have) been notified of the change in schedule.

b. Everyone (is/are) brining a homemade dish.

c. One of the speakers (is/are) not here yet.

d. Neither of the cars in the accident (was/were) insured.

e. Most of the rooms in the hotels (have/has (air-conditioning.

2. **Identify each verb as active or passive**

   a. The letter was obviously singed by the director.

   ………………………………………………………..

   b. Most of the books have been chosen by the professors.

   …………………………………………………………

   c. I try to watch as little television as possible.

   …………………………………………………………

   d. The air conditioner was delivered later in the day.

   ………………………………………………………..

   e. The judge suddenly called the lawyers into her chamber.

   ………………………………………………………….

   f. The patient was being taken by ambulance to the plane

   ………………………………………………………..

   g. A decaying tooth was extracted by my dentist.

   ………………………………………………………..

   h. The secretary opens the mail.

   …………………………………………………………

   i. My wallet was stolen.

   ………………………………………………………….

PART THREE

1. **Answer the following questions briefly:**

   a. Disuses the three major differences between active and passive voice.

   b. Disuses the main forms of the passive verb phrase.

   c. Write a short essay on the two main kinds of verb.

2. Spot the mistake and then write the correct one:-

- The jury are giving their verdict now.

....

- The jury is giving its verdict now.

....

- The jury is arguing among itself.

....

- The jury are arguing among themselves.

....

- The visiting team are to defend the west goal.

....

- The visiting team is to defend the west goal.

....

CHAPTER FOUR

ADJECTIVE & ADVERB IN ENGLISH

The gift of language is the single of human trait that narks us all genetically, setting us apart from the rest of life.

Lewis Thomas, the lives of a Cell

4.1 Defining an Adjective.

An adjective can be defined as :

a. A word used to describe a noun or pronoun or to give a noun or pronoun a more specific meaning.

b. A word that modifies the meaning of a substance.

c. A word that qualifies a noun adds to its meaning but limits its application. Mitchell :1994:11)

d. Qualifies of nouns; that is to say they describe or indicate the person or thing denoted by the noun.

e. Any word which is an expansion of the English grammatical category adjective in an English grammar, or a transformational replacement of such a word.(Palmer: 1990:12)

f. A class of lexical words identified by their ability to fill the following two positions (1) between noun-determiner and non, and (2) immediately following the function word (very). Thomas: 1997:90)

g. A word that modifies a noun and also exhibits certain formal characteristics which distinguish it from the noun class; lack of a plural form, capacity for being compared or for being itself modified by words like extremely, beautifully, somewhat, attachment of certain suffix like{-y,-en,-able}.(Roberts (1981:70).

4.2 Characteristics of Adjectives.

Adjectives are words that describe the thing, quality, state, or action which a noun refers to. In English, adjectives usually have the following characteristics (Quirk,ibid.,114):

a. They can freely occur in attributive position, i.e., they can premodify a noun, e.g., clever as in:

-The clever student answers the question prudently.

b. They can freely occur in predicative position, i.e., they can function as: wise/ugly.

-This old man seems wise.

(Subject complement)

-She made her patents happy.

(Object complement)

c. They can be premodified by the intensifier very as:

- Dr. Ali is very competent in translation.

d. They can take comparative and superlative forms, whether inflectionally, i.e.,{-er} or{-est} as in:

- Which is the warmer of the two countries? Saudi Arabia or Sudan.?

- Which the warmest of the three countries? Saudi   Arabia, Sudan or India?

4.3   Properties of Adjectives.

R. Richard at al (1bid,8) listed the following properties of English adjectives:-

   i. They can be used before a noun, **e.g.**, a <u>heavy</u> bag.
  ii. They can be used after {be, become, seem, etc., as complement, **e.g.**, the bag <u>is heavy</u>.
 iii. They can be used after a noun as a complement, **e.g.**, these books make the bag <u>heavy.</u>
  iv. They can be modified by an adverb, **e.g.**, a<u> very</u> heavy bag.
   v. They can be used in a comparative or superlative form, **e.g.**, the bag seems <u>heavier</u> now.

4.4   Syntactic subclassifcation of Adjectives:

(Quirk,ibid.,121) states that adjectives can be subclassified into the following three functions:

   a. both attributive and predicative ,**e.g.**, a <u>hungry</u> man. The man is <u>hungry</u>.
   b. Attributive only**, e.g.**, an utter fool. *The fool is utter.
   c. Predicative only**, e.g.**, *a <u>loath</u> woman. The woman is <u>loath</u> to admit.

4.5   Adjectives phrases .

An Adjectives phrase can be defined as:

   a. A phrase used to modify nouns or pronouns.
   b. A phrase that functions as an adjective.
   c. A propositional phrase that modifies a noun or pronoun by telling what kind or which one.

Jacobs(ibi.,p.106) pointed out that: adjective phrases usually modify nouns functions as subject, direct object, indirect object, or predicate nominatives

Noun functions	Adjective phrase
Modifying a subject.	The <u>mansion across</u> the road has been abandoned
Modifying a direct object.	Ali quickly erased the <u>poem on</u> the board .
Modifying a indirect object.	A realtor sold the descent neighbors <u>above</u> us a new house.
Modifying a predicate nominative	A unicorn is a gentle whit <u>creature with</u> a single horn.

4.6 Features of Adjectives phrases.

Praninskas (1990:120) states the following features of adjective phrases concerning:

a) **Form:**

The adjective phrases consist of a preposition and a noun with or without modifiers: **,e.g.**, the bend <u>in the delta</u>

b) **Order :**

In contrast with single word adjectives, phrases follow the words they modify. **,e.g.**, a <u>tall</u> man <u>with a gray hair</u>.

c) **Agreement :**

The verb of a sentence or clause agrees in number with the subject noun which is modified and not with a noun in the modifying phrase. **e.g.**, that book of short stories <u>is</u> hers.

d) Definite Article (The) :

When an adjective phrases limits the meaning of the noun it modifies to one specific instance, the noun is preceded by the.

e.g., the books for Graphology are very expensive

4.7   Adjectives clauses.

An adjective clause can be defined as:

a. A subordinate clause that modifies a noun or profound by telling what kind or which one.
b. A clause that follows and modifies a noun headword or a pronoun.
c. Dependent clauses, usually introduced by relative pronouns which serve as subordinating connectives who, whom, whose, which, and that.

Sometimes, however, adjective clauses may begin with a relative adverb, such as before, since, when, where, or why. All of these words relate the clause to the word it modifies.

Adjective clauses begin with relative pronouns or relative adverbs.

E.g.,

1. Anyone who remains calm will probably be good in an emergency.
2. I finished reading the book that you loaned me.
3. We gave the stray mutt, which we found, a hearty meal.
4. Spring is the time when peepers make their shrill evening sound.

5. Our trip to Jazan ended with a visit to the <u>village where</u> my parents were born

4.8 Restrictive and Non- Restrictive Adjectives clauses.

Adjective clauses can be divided into two types;-

a. **Restrictive Adjectives clause**:- is one that is essential in defining or limiting a noun or a pronoun.
b. **Non-Restrictive Adjectives clause**:- is one that is not essential in defining or limiting a noun or a pronoun.(Murphy.1997:102)

E.g.,

1. The students who had participated in extra- circular activities were given honorary certificates (restrictive clause)
2. The students, who had participated in extra- circular activities were given honorary certificates (Non restrictive or appositive)

4.9 Adverbs.

Adverbs can be defined as:-

a. A word that modifies a verb, an adjective, or another a Adverb.
b. A word that describes or adds to the meaning of a verb, an adjective, another adverb, or a sentence, and which answers such questions as how?, Where?, or When.?

Examples of adverbs

a. Our new teacher greeted us **<u>warmly</u>**.(**manner**).
b. How long has he lived **<u>here?(place</u>**).
c. We arrived early **<u>last night.(time</u>**).

d. Well, I hope you'll be **really** happy.**(degree)**

e. After that we met him quite **frequently(frequency)** .

f. **However**, we learned very little about her.**(linking).**

g. **Strangely,** they never talked about him.**(comment and attitude).**

h. She talked **only** about us and the college (adding **and limiting).**

i. **Personally**, I found that annoying.**(viewpoint)** .

j. Have you **ever** met anyone like that? (**Length of time).**

4.10   Characteristics of Adverbs.

The most common Characteristics of the adverb is morphological: the majority of adverbs have the derivational suffix {-ly}.

There are two types of syntactic function that characterize adverbs, but an adverb need have only one of these:

1. Adverbial

Adverbial is divided into the following three classes:-

a. **Adjuncts** : are integrated within the structure of the clause to at least some extent. **E.g.,**
   - They are waiting outside.
   - I can now understand it.
   - He spoke to me about it frankly.

b. **Disjuncts & Conjuncts:** are not integrated within the clause. Semantically, Disjuncts express an evaluation of what is being said either with respect to the form of the communication or to its content.
   E.g.,.

- <u>Frankly</u> I am tired.
- <u>Fortunately,</u> no one complained.
- They are <u>probably</u> at home.

4.11   Adverb Clauses.

Subordinate adverb clauses modify verbs, adjectives, adverbs, or verbals by telling where, when, in what manner, to what extent, under what condition, or why.

All adverb clauses begin with Subordinating conjunctions

Functions	Adverb clauses
Modifying a verb	When the fog is <u>dense,</u> you should <u>use</u> low beans.
Modifying an adjective	Dr. Ali seemed <u>happy whenever</u> he was.
Modifying an adverb	<u>Faster than</u> the eye could follow, the race car sped away.
Modifying a participle	<u>Laughing until</u> he gasped for breath, Ali cold not speak.
Modifying a gerund	<u>Driving</u> a car <u>if you</u> do not have a license.
Modifying an infinitive	We decided to <u>remain</u> in our seats <u>so</u> that we could watch the movie again.

Practical Exercise (4)

PART ONE

1.Spot the mistake and then write the correct one:-

a. Erosion is where the soil is washed away.

....

b. Illiteracy is when a man cannot read or write.

....

c. This is the reason why I am working.

....

d. Why did you he go to Europe during the summer?

....

e. The team played really well for the first five minutes.

....

f. He played well in every game.

....

g. She decided to work slow and easy.

....

h. My greatest thirst comes when I work hard in a strong sun.

....

i. Now is the time when he should be on hand.

....

j. What did you paint the house white for?

....

2.Write the adjective clause in each of the following sentence

a. The student whom Dr. Ali chose was first in his class.

……………………………………………………………………

b. My father works in an office where everyone helps each other.

…………………………………………………………..………...

c. The position that Dr.Sameeh wanted was already filled.

…………………………………………………….………………

d. Our University played, which lasted two hours, was enjoyed by everyone.

…………….………………………………………...………...

i. A student who studies regularly finds test-taking easy.

……………………………………………………………………

PART TWO

1. Choose the correct form in these sentences

a. This apple tastes (sweet/sweetly).

……………………………………………………………..

b. He spoke to (plain/plainly).

……………………………………………………………….

c. The baby would not stay (quietly/ quiet).

………………………………………………………………….

d. We will be leaving (shortly/short).

……………………………………………………………….

e. The weather never turns (cold/coldly).

………………………………………………………………….

2. Write the adjective phrase or phrases in each of the following sentence

a. His masterpiece is a book of with three parts.

……………………………………………………………..

b. Some of the student in my class showed interest in translation.

……………………………………………………………….

c.   The lecture about Saudi folklore is fascinating.

…………………………………………………………………

d. The wind blew down the tree on the corner of the block.

………………………………………………………………..

e. Ali' teacher wrote a not for her son's absence.

……………………………………………………………….

PART THREE

1. Change the underlined phrases in these sentences into two- word combinations.

a.   A play which has three acts.

…………………………………………………………..

b. A building which has thirty floors.

…………………………………………………………………

c.   A teacher who teaches English.

………………………………………………………………….

d. A store which sells shoes.

………………………………………………………………….

e. A student who studies science .

………………………………………………………………

2. Complete these sentences with the correct form of the adjectives in parentheses :

a.   The less she works,(happy) she is.

………………………………………………………………….

b. The bigger the car, (fast) you can go.

…………………………………………………………………..

c. (Fresh) it is,(good) it will taste.

    …………………………………………………………..

d. (More) you eat, (fat) you will get.

    …………………………………………………………

e. It was becoming (cold) and (cold).

    …………………………………………………………

SELECTEDBIBLIOGRAPHY

- Ag, Ben. 1992 the Discourse of Domination: From the Frankfurt school to Postmodernism. Evanston: North western University press.

- Allen, J. Chomsky: *Selected Readings* Oxford: University Press.1971.

- …………………….. *Syntactic Structure*. Oxford: University Press.1971.

- Adams,V.(1971) *Introduction to Modern English Word- Formation.* London .

- Anserson, J.(1981). *The Grammar of Case*. Cambridge.

- Al.Bashir, Ali. (2008) *Semantics*. Kingdom of Saudi Arabia.

- A, Louses. (1971). *Ideology and Ideological State App*aratus: London: New left Books.

- Austin, John L. (1962). How to do things with a words. Oxford: Oxford University Press.

- Bach,E. (1996) *Universal in Linguistics Theory*. New York.

- Bauman, Richard; and Joel Shizer (ed) (1974). *Explorations in Ethnography of Speaking.* Cambridge: Cambridge University Press.

- Bateson, Gregory. (1972). *Steps to an Ecology of Mind*. New York: Ballantine.

- Beaugrande, Robert- Alain de; and Wolfgang U. Dresslter. (1981). *Introduction to Text linguistics*, London. Longman.

- Bell, Allam; and Peter Garrett(eds.)(1997) Approaches to Media Discourse. Oxford: Black well.

- Bloomfiedl. Leaonard. (1933) Language. New York; Holt.

- Bukher, Karl. (1965): Dialogue and Discourse . A sociolinguistic Approach to Modern Drama Dialogue and Naturally Occurring Conversation. London

- CloseR. and et al. (199): Texts and Practices: Readings in Critical Discourse Analysis: London: Rout ledge.

- Cheapen, Christine. (1966). the Predictability of Informal conversation. London: Printer.

- Chomsky, G. (1997).Aspects of the Theory of Syntax. London.

- Clark, Herbet H.(1990). Using language Chicago: University of Chicago press.

- Coates, Jennitier. (1996) Women Talk. Oxford: Black well.

- ....(ed) (1998).Language and Gender. A reader . Oxford: Blackwel.

- Malcolm.(1977) Introduction to Discourse analysis. London Rout ledge.

- ......(ed) (1992). Advances in spoken discourse analysis. London: Rout ledge.

- Crystal, David. (2001).Language and the Internet. Cambridge: Cambridge University Press.

- ………….,(1991) <u>Investigating English Style.</u> London

- Dessler, Richard A; and Roger J. Kreuz. (2000).<u>Transcribing oral Discourse: A Survey and mode (system.</u> Discourse processes 29. 25 – 76.

- Edwards, Derek. (1997). <u> Discourse and Cognition.</u> London : sage .

- Eggins, Suzanne, and Diana Slade. (1997). <u> Analyzing Casual Conversation</u> London : Chassell.

- Fair Clough, Norman. L. (1989). <u> Language and Power.</u> London : Longman.

- ………,(1997) <u>Discourse and Social Change.</u> Cambridge: polity .

- Fasold, Ralph. (1990) <u> Sociolinguistic of Language.</u> Oxford: Black well.

- Firth, Alan, (199). <u> The Discourses of Negotiation.</u> Oxford.

- ………, 1973. <u>Papers in Linguistics,</u> 1934 – 1951- London : Oxford University Press.

- Fowler, Roger. (1991). <u>Language and Control.</u> London : Rout ledge.

- Fox, Batsara. (1987). <u> Discourse Structure and Anaphora.</u> Cambridge: Cambridge University Press.

- Gazdar, Gerald. (1979).<u>Pragmatics, Implicative, Presupposition, and Logical Eorrs..</u> New York: Academic

- Gee.K.(1999) <u>An Introduction to Discourses Analysis.</u> London: Rout ledge.

- Gilas, Howard, et al. (1991). <u>Language Context and Consequence.</u> Milton Keynes: Open University Press.

- Goddard, Angela, et al. (1997) <u>Language and Genders..</u> London: .

- Gottmann, Evving. (1967) . <u>Forms of Talk.</u> Oxford : Blackwell.

- Gregory, Michael. (1967): <u>Language and Situation.</u> London: Rout ledge.

- Frice, H. Raul. (1957) <u>Meaning Philosophical Review .</u> 377 .

- Gunnarsson, Britt. Louise, et al. (1990). <u>The construction of professional discourse.</u> London : Longman.

- Halliday, M.A.K. (1976).<u>System and Function in Language</u>. London : Oxford University Press.

- ......, (1974). <u>Language as Social Semantic</u> London : E/ Arnold.

- ...., in SRH Asan (1976.)<u> Cohesion </u> in <u>English.</u> London : Longman.

- .... SR Hasan. (1969).<u>Language Context, and Text.</u> Oxford: Oxford University Press.

- Heath, Shirley Brie. (1983). <u>Ways with Words.</u> London: Cambridge University Press.

- Hoey, Michacl. (2001). <u>Textual Interaction: an Introduction to Written Discourse Analysis.</u> London Routlege.

- Leech, G. (1997) <u>*the Grammar of English Nominalization.*</u> Indiana

- Lyons.(1968) <u>*Introduction to Theoretical Linguistics.*</u>

- Cambridge

- Palmer, F.R(1973) *The English Verb*. London.

Postal P.(1968) *Morphology*. London.

- ……………(1970) Syntax. London.

- Quirk, R et al, (1998) *A Grammar of Contemporary English*. Longman.

- Robins, R.H.(1965). *General Linguistics*. Longman.

- Thakur.M(2000). *Morphology*. India.

- ……………..(2000) *Syntax*, India.

- Turner, G.W.*(19973) Styptics*. Harmondsworth

- Sweet, H.(1981) *The Practical Study of Language*. Oxford.

- Wells, R.S (1986) *Syntax.* Cambridge: Cambridge University Press.